independent and works with a wide range of partners of all political persuasions and none.

Fabian Society
61 Petty France
London SW1H 9EU
www.fabians.org.uk

Fabian Ideas 640

First published 2015
ISBN 978-0-7163-0640-5

Editorial Director: Ed Wallis

British Library Cataloguing in Publication data. A catalogue record for this book is available from the British Library.

Printed and bound by DG3, London, UK

To find out more about the Fabian Society, the Young Fabians, the Fabian Women's Network and our local societies, please visit our web site at www.fabians.org.uk.

Tax for our Times

How the left can reinvent taxation

Edited by Daisy-Rose Srblin

About the Friedrich-Ebert-Stiftung

The Friedrich-Ebert-Stiftung is a non-profit German political foundation committed to the advancement of public policy issues in the spirit of the basic values of social democracy through research, education, and international cooperation.

The FES, headquartered in Berlin and Bonn, has 13 regional offices throughout Germany and maintains an international network of offices in more than 100 countries.

FRIEDRICH EBERT STIFTUNG

Friedrich-Ebert-Stiftung
44 Charlotte Street, London W1T 2NR
T: +44 (0)207 612 1900
E: info@feslondon.net
www.feslondon.org.uk

About the Authors

Fran Bennett is a senior research and teaching fellow in the Department of Social Policy and Intervention at the University of Oxford, and an independent consultant. She writes in a personal capacity.

Adam Corlett is economic analyst at the Resolution Foundation where he works on the labour market, fiscal policy and tax and welfare.

Patrick Diamond is lecturer in Public Policy at Queen Mary, University of London, and vice-chair and research director at Policy Network.

Howard Glennerster is emeritus professor of social policy and an associate at the Centre for Analysis of Social Exclusion at the London School of Economics.

Andrew Harrop is general secretary of the Fabian Society.

Richard Murphy is director of Tax Research LLP, and is an adviser to the Tax Justice Network and the Trade Union Congress on taxation and economic issues.

Faiza Shaheen is head of inequality and sustainable development at Save the Children.

Beck Smith is private sector adviser at Save the Children.

Daisy-Rose Srblin is research fellow at the Fabian Society and leads the Future of Tax programme.

Ulrich Storck is director of FES London.

Tony Travers is professor in the Department of Government at LSE and director of LSE London. He served as chair of the London Finance Commission.

A discussion could address some or all of the following questions:

1. What are the most significant lessons the UK can learn from the continent and from international experience on tax reform? In what ways is the UK idiosyncratic when compared to other countries?

2. What is the role of government and politicians in engaging the public with this debate? How can a technical subject like tax be spoken about in a more open and accessible way?

3. What does the scope for radical tax reform look like over the course of the next parliament?

Please let us know what you think

Whatever view you take of the issues, we would very much like to hear about your discussion. Please send us a summary of your debate (perhaps 300 words) to debate@fabians.org.uk.

A Convenient Truth

A Better Society for Us and the Planet

Richard Wilkinson and Kate Pickett

In 'A Convenient Truth' Richard Wilkinson and Kate Pickett set out a path towards a society that's better for us and the planet. Inequality drives status insecurity, which fuels the consumerism that is destroying our planet. But the things we buy aren't making us any happier: the link between economic development and real improvements in quality of life is broken in rich societies.

For real improvements in wellbeing, we need a more equal society, which is best achieved by putting democracy at the heart of the economy. Indeed, the authors see the extension of democracy into economic institutions as the next major step in the long project of human emancipation.

JOIN THE FABIANS TODAY

Join us and receive at least four pamphlets or books a year as well as our quarterly magazine, 'Fabian Review'.

I'd like to become a Fabian

Standard Rate: £3.50 per month/£42 per annum
Reduced Rate (unwaged): £1.75 per month/£21 per annum

Name	Date of birth
Address	Postcode
Email	
Telephone	

Instruction to Bank

Originator's ID: 971666

DIRECT Debit

Bank/building society name	
Address	
Acct holder(s)	Postcode
Acct no.	Sort code

I instruct you to pay direct debits from my account at the request of the Fabian Society. The instruction is subject to the safeguards of the Direct Debit Guarantee.

Signature	Date

Return to:
Fabian Society Membership
FREEPOST RTEG – XLTU – AEJX
61 Petty France, London SW1H 9EU

Acknowledgements

First and foremost, sincere thanks to the Friedrich-Ebert-Stiftung for their co-operation on this project.

I am very grateful to Fran Bennett, Adam Corlett, Patrick Diamond, Howard Glennerster, Andrew Harrop, Ann Mumford, Richard Murphy, Faiza Shaheen, Beck Smith and Tony Travers for their contributions to the collection. Thanks also to those who attended our expert seminar at the beginning of the project, which helped to shape the scope of this collection.

Particular thanks also go to Ed Wallis for all his help and guidance over the course of this project. Fabian Society staff as always offered support and motivation throughout, in different ways.

Lastly, an extended special thanks to the Barry Amiel & Norman Melburn Trust for generously funding a year-long research fellowship at the Fabian Society, allowing me to undertake this work.

CONTENTS

Foreword xi

Introduction 1
Daisy-Rose Srblin

1: Tax after the crisis 7
Patrick Diamond

2: A hyper-centralised anomaly 17
Tony Travers

3: Institutional interests 25
Richard Murphy

4: Global tax avoidance 31
Faiza Shaheen and Beck Smith

5: Something for something 37
Andrew Harrop

National insurance: a case study 44
Fran Bennett

6: On the margins 47
Ann Mumford

7: A wealth of options 55
Howard Glennerster

8: Poorly targeted 63
Adam Corlett

FOREWORD

Tax is a word that hardly ever carries positive connotations. The common use of the term "taxpayer" sometimes seems to reduce the citizen to a technical subject for the functioning of the state. In German, the word "Steuerverschwendung" (meaning 'the waste of taxes') is often used for contested public projects or state activities. Indeed, in 2000, the Fabian Society's Commission on Tax and Citizenship stated "of course, taxes will never be popular". This statement has stood the test of time: tax and its reform has maintained its toxic reputation as a perceived vote loser.

Tax is still seen as a political taboo: yet, it remains a cornerstone in the relationship between the citizen and the state in a representative democracy. However, in the years since the Commission's report *Paying for Progress*, much has changed in the public discourse around tax. In particular, the global financial crisis and the exposure of the long-standing practice of tax avoidance by large multi-national corporations, has brought home the international dimension to the debate. Taxation was once the exclusive domain of national sovereignty, but as the example of the Luxembourg tax files (where an EU member state legally enabled tax avoidance, to the detriment of revenue in a range of nations) indicates, tax avoidance is now more than ever a matter of European and international concern and action. In the context of increasingly interdependent economies and societies, taxes can no longer be seen in the single national context: they pose international challenges too. The intention of taxing international financial transactions is an obvious example of connecting tax collection on the international level.

Hence there are new preconditions for a debate on profound tax reforms, in the UK as well as in other countries like Germany. Although tax policy in the European countries has followed a trend in recent years away from taxing labour by increasing taxes on consumption and properties, distributional objectives and fairness have often been lacking. This debate should be led by centre-left values, asking the crucial question of how to use tax policies to balance wealth distribution, counteract inequality and ultimately reorganise the relationship between state and citizens in a globalised world. At the same time, reforms need to have popular appeal without seeming piecemeal or hinging on a single issue.

This collection of essays outlines in an accessible manner some of the areas where such reforms are needed and could be possible, always taking into account the international perspective and experiences from other countries where significant. Creating a fairer, more effective tax system is a challenge for progressive forces across Europe.

Building on previous work by both the Friedrich-Ebert-Stiftung and the Fabian Society, we hope to provide an inspiring contribution to a necessary debate that is fundamental to the goal of all progressives across Europe: creating a more equal society.

Ulrich Storck
Director, Friedrich-Ebert-Stiftung London

INTRODUCTION

Daisy-Rose Srblin

The UK's tax system isn't fit for purpose and specialists across the board agree on the need for reform.

The Institute for Fiscal Studies' Mirrlees Review provided a comprehensive evaluation of the tax system, stressing its complexity and arguing that there is an urgent need for the simplification of a tax code that currently numbers 21,000 pages. It was hailed by experts upon publication. Yet its findings and message were largely ignored by politicians across party lines, with sensible reforms being overlooked in the interests of short-term electioneering.

Aside from the heavy technical analysis too often associated with debates about tax, we urgently need a political conversation about tax reform, which considers *how* we tax as well as *how much*. The Fabian Society Commission on Taxation and Citizenship of 2000 and the more recent *Values Added: Rethinking Tax for the Twentieth-Century*, both set out a number of principles to strengthen the popular legitimacy of tax, as well as making it more progressive, more transparent and more efficient. Indeed, such principles are in line with public opinion, with 96 per cent of people wanting to see a more progressive tax system, according to the Equality Trust. Throughout the recent election campaign, polling seemed to suggest public appetite for more progressive forms of taxation, from support for the 'Mansion' Tax to an endorsement of small increases in personal taxes to fund health and social care spending.

But political action has not been taken in line with these values. Instead, tax breaks for the wealthiest have been prioritised over support for families with children, the working poor and those reliant on welfare. George Osborne's 'tax lock' effectively puts 60 per cent of all taxation revenue out of reach for the duration of the new parliament: income tax, national insurance and VAT. In general, it seems that the public only gets a political discussion on tax when taxes are getting cut.

Furthermore, the tax system remains far from progressive. The most recent Office for National Statistics figures show that the poorest 10 per cent pay 45p in every pound of their income in tax, while the richest 10 per cent pay only 35p in every pound. Council tax remains distinctly regressive, with individuals occupying properties of vastly different values expected to pay roughly the same amount in taxation. The Resolution Foundation has demonstrated that extensions in the personal allowance are not only misleading in their presentation as 'lifting people out of tax', given that most low earners continue to be liable for national insurance contributions, but they also disproportionately benefit higher earners. We are moving towards a less progressive system, to the detriment of the many for the benefit of the few.

The public should be at the heart of debates about tax, but so far they have been crowded out by technocratic, and seemingly apolitical, contributions dominated by highly-qualified specialists. The failure of politicians to engage with the issue means we've yet to find a way to talk about tax that is open and accessible, enabling a conversation that we can all understand, one inspired by political values.

The left needs to fight for a tax system that treats the poorest more fairly, and fight to re-establish the principle of redistribution. Inequality suppresses productivity and increases economic instability. Conversely, a redistributive tax and benefits system will enhance social mobility, allowing people to fulfil their potential by creating a level-playing field. The left must push for this vision of society, defending the progressive purpose for taxation, and shaping its future reform by making tax debates less technocratic and more publicly accessible. The essays in this collection demonstrate how tax reform can be engaging: in sum, they outline practical proposals setting out how the left can build a tax system fit for modern times.

In chapter one, Patrick Diamond argues this requires reasserting the salience of tax as a means of redistribution, as well as for fiscal consolidation. For Tony Travers in chapter two, it is time that Britain's hyper-centralised system learnt from its European counterparts and dispersed tax raising powers to cities and regions. Richard Murphy in chapter three thinks we must take on the vested institutional interests that allow policy-making to serve multinational corporations rather than ordinary taxpayers. Faiza Shaheen and Beck Smith in chapter four powerfully argue that the progressive global tax justice movement must avoid complacency when it comes to achievements on tackling tax avoidance, to fight for the position of developing countries in decision-making, and defend the moral case for paying tax to avoid a global 'race to the bottom' on tax rates. And Andrew Harrop argues in chapter five that our constrained public finances compel us to strengthen the link between taxes paid and revenue spent, not least in the interests of increasing spending on health and social care, and that this may involve learning lessons from social insurance systems on the continent. Fran Bennett also makes the case for a rejuvenated national insurance system in her case study.

As well as institutional reform, there is also a need to reconceptualise the principles and purposes of the tax system. Ann Mumford argues in chapter six that inequalities of capital need to be seen in gender as well as income terms: the left must remember that gender rights are not all about identity politics, but also concern the gendered distribution of wealth in society. Indeed, as the UK Women's Budget Group stated after the summer budget: 'The majority of people losing from cuts to tax credits will be women and the majority of people gaining from rising tax thresholds will be men'. The left also needs to commit itself to shifting the burden of taxation away from earned income and on to wealth, where inequalities are far greater, in order to tax property and assets far more effectively, as Howard Glennerster stresses in chapter seven. Finally, government must commit itself to lowering the tax burdens on low income families properly, by reforming national insurance (presently paid by many who are not liable to pay income tax) and indirect duties that unfairly hit the poorest hardest, as examined by Adam Corlett in chapter eight.

Crucially, tax is no longer a question within national borders, and this collection draws on international comparisons throughout. Challenges such as tackling the tax avoidance of multi-nationals require coordinated action across institutions, and the UK needs to look beyond its own borders to understand how models such as fiscal devolution might work here. Indeed, arguably the hardest ask of all, the European left must work in solidarity to pursue reforms in favour of greater wealth taxation, and easing tax burdens on lower income groups, in order to re-establish the importance of using tax as a distributional mechanism. Tax reforms with a strong social democratic impulse will only gain real political salience, and have real impact, should they follow a concerted movement across nations in the interests of fairness.

This collection offers both practical reforms and new perspectives, from giving HMRC ministerial representation and responsibility to recognising the legitimacy of feminism within tax debates. But reform must go hand in hand with creating a tax system that is legitimate in the eyes of the public. For too long, tax has been perceived as politically toxic. Yet polling throughout the election suggested that when spoken of in the right way, the public does not necessarily dislike talking about tax.

As such, more needs to be done to connect the payment of taxes to the funding of strong, popular services.

Furthermore, politicians must be properly accountable to their public, providing readable, clear and understandable information about the taxes each citizen pays, how much each contributes, and how government revenue is being used.

Conducting a conversation about tax reform without the public, which pays the revenue, does not make sense. Tax reform should neither be locked away by politicians from public view, nor left to the expert few: it needs to be put back in the hands of the many.

1: TAX AFTER THE CRISIS: UK AND EU TAX POLICY SINCE 2008

Patrick Diamond

Recent tax reforms across Europe have been both broadly sensible and consistent with a progressive framework of fiscal policy and macro-economic management. However, achieving equity and fairness have been significantly downplayed. A major task for social democrats is to ensure the tax system achieves the progressive goal of constraining the increase in relative differences between the top and bottom.

In recent years the focus of fiscal policy in the UK, as in many industrialised countries in the wake of the financial crisis, has been on reducing the overall rate of public expenditure. However, despite a series of reforms to reduce tax avoidance and fraud, the tax system has largely remained unchanged since 2008, despite major concerns about its underlying resilience. Under the coalition government after 2010, the policy priority was radically curtailing spending rather than improving the sustainability of UK tax revenues. This was a major policy error reflecting a basic misunderstanding of what caused the financial crash and the ensuing fiscal crisis, no doubt encouraged by Conservative politicians after 2008.

Britain's weak public finances and rising levels of public debt were not primarily created by profligacy and overspending in the New Labour years. Instead it was the absence of a more resilient tax system and an over-reliance on tax revenues generated from the deregulated financial services sector. As the crisis struck and financial services' activity was squeezed, tax revenues fell dramatically, leaving the UK among the most exposed of the advanced economies. Although the Labour governments between 1997 and 2010 simplified the tax system and reduced the burden of corporate taxation as a means of promoting global competitiveness, too little consideration had been given to the likely impact of external macro-economic shocks on the UK's tax base. This was unquestionably a serious failing of Labour's macro-economic policy regime.

These events are a reminder that progressive centre-left parties have a variety of tax reform principles that they ought to achieve. The tax system is not only a means of raising resources to pay for vital public services while redistributing income between those on higher and lower incomes: it is also concerned with maximising stability and resilience in revenues, avoiding the 'boom and bust' scenario which ensued after the financial crash in the UK. As such, an important political challenge is to strengthen public legitimacy and confidence in the tax state after a long period in which tax resistance among UK voters has apparently been growing. There is a particular need to broaden the scope of taxation beyond 'earned' income to property, consumption, and activities which have a negative impact on the environment. Indeed, Britain can learn much from the reforms introduced by other European countries since the financial crisis.

Tax reform across EU member-states

According to the European Commission, taxation policies in EU member-states since 2010 have focused on advancing three broad public policy objectives: ensuring more sustainable public finances in the wake of the crash; promoting rather than inhibiting economic growth and employment after a prolonged recession and contraction of aggregate demand; and shaping fairer distributional outcomes as a countervailing force against rising market-based inequalities over recent decades. European countries have generally been effective since the 1990s at using tax and benefits systems to contain the rise in income inequalities, but there has been considerable reluctance to use the tax system to constrain the inexorable increase in top incomes. In 2011, the Organisation for Economic Co-operation and Development (OECD) warned that, "from the mid-1990s to 2005, the reduced redistributive capacity of tax-benefit systems was sometimes the main source of widening household-income gaps".

There are a number of discernible trends in tax reform across the EU since 2010, outlined in a recent survey report by the European Commission. First, the tax burden has been rising across Europe as member-states seek to consolidate their public finances in the wake of the financial crash, although the Commission expects this to stabilise in the years ahead. The UK's tax burden is lower than most other European countries: here, tax revenues are 32.9 per cent of national income, whereas the average across Western Europe is currently 38.9 per cent.

Secondly, there has been a sustained effort to reduce the burden of taxation on employment and labour. Measures have been targeted on low income groups, in particular in the more vulnerable sectors of the labour market. The Commission notes that there has historically been a "relatively high" tax burden on labour in Europe: reducing taxes on workers is designed not only to promote employment and job creation but to ease the pressures on low income households in the wake of the financial crisis. According to the Commission's study, a small number of member-states such as Belgium and Slovakia have reduced taxes on employers, encouraging them to hire workers 'on the margins' of the labour market, notably disabled people and the long-term unemployed. Measures have not only lessened the cumulative burden of taxation on labour, but have been used to cut taxes for the lowest paid through tax credits and higher allowances. Moreover, in the wake of the financial crisis, a number of measures were taken to increase the tax burden for high earners particularly in the financial sector. However, this wave of reforms has now, the Commission says, "run its course" and further tax increases on the rich have been rare, not only in the UK. A number of countries have sought to identify alternative sources of revenue, enabling them to cut labour taxes without having a detrimental impact on public finances.

The third trend has therefore been a willingness to increase taxes on consumption either by increasing tax rates or by broadening the tax base. Consumption taxes tend to be favoured because they have less discernible impact on economic growth, and usually provide a more stable source of revenue. Understandably, there has also been a focus on taxing 'bads' such as alcohol and tobacco consumption, not only to increase revenues but to alter consumer behaviour and to promote public health objectives: countries from Poland to the Netherlands, as well as the UK, are increasing excise duties on these goods.

Fourth, a number of member-states have increased environmental taxes, although the impact of these additional revenues on the public finances has so far been modest. The aim of environmental taxes is to meet stated EU objectives relating to carbon use and climate change, such as reducing the use of fossil fuels by altering the behaviour of businesses and consumers.

Fifth, there has been some willingness to increase taxes on property, although this is by no means common to all member-states. Taxes on 'immovable property' are considered to be least harmful to growth and produce fewer distortions than taxes on property transactions, but such taxes presently account for only 3.8 per cent of tax revenues across the EU, as the Commission notes. A number of member-states have continued to offer tax relief on mortgage interest payments, but many are reviewing these arrangements given the tendency to increase household indebtedness and to inflate the housing market increasing the risk of financial instability, as well as the regressive nature of such tax deductions. In the UK, for example, the housing market continues to be distorted by tax reliefs on 'buy-to-let' properties.

Sixth, member-states including France and Spain have used the tax system in order to stimulate 'entrepreneurial activity', for example by increasing incentives for equity investment in unquoted companies, as well as offering tax deductions on capital gains for individuals purchasing shares in start-up SMEs, such as the reforms recently introduced in Sweden. The UK has taken further steps to increase investment allowances for business.

Finally, all countries have been making sustained efforts to improve 'tax governance', strengthening tax compliance and reducing tax evasion, balancing these measures to encourage voluntary compliance with policies to strengthen enforcement. The European Commission emphasises that one of the most important steps in improving the resilience of the tax system in member-states has been to broaden the tax base, while reducing the number of tax exemptions which tend to have distortive effects on economic decision-making by households and firms. What these various tax reform principles illustrate, as Tony Atkinson notes in his recent book, *Inequality: What can be done?*, is that despite the constraints imposed by globalisation, national governments can, and do, continue to make discretionary choices about the structure of the tax system with major implications for equity and efficiency in their respective countries.

Principles of tax reform

After 2010, the coalition government in the UK focused on the following priorities for tax reform: raising VAT rates, extending the tax free personal allowance, cutting income tax for the highest earners, reducing business taxes, increasing taxes on property transactions at the upper end of the housing market, and strengthening measures to tackle tax evasion and avoidance. As can be seen from the discussion above, this direction of travel was broadly consistent with tax reforms across numerous EU member-states. However, George Osborne has continued the process of weakening the tax base by raising the threshold for the starting rate of tax. This is very costly and does not help the low paid as much as the better off. At the same time, the chancellor has cut corporation tax, believing that a national strategy of tax competition is right for the UK. This is somewhat at odds with the much bolder efforts by the previous Labour government to curb tax avoidance and build support for co-ordinated international action.

After 2015, it appears likely that a number of tax reform principles will continue to have salience across Europe. The first will be improving the resilience of tax systems in order to complete the task of fiscal consolidation. Second, we are likely to see a further shift away from taxing labour by increasing taxes on consumption and 'immovable property'. Third, the tax system will be used to stimulate entrepreneurial activity and small business formation. And, fourth, will be the use of environmental taxes to alter the long-term behaviour of citizens, businesses and key actors throughout the economy.

These general principles of tax reform appear at first sight to be broadly sensible and consistent with a progressive framework of fiscal policy and macro-economic management. In particular, the emphasis on reducing the taxation burden on labour is consistent both with promoting employment and raising living standards across the income distribution. What is striking, nonetheless, is the relatively low salience of reform principles relating to the distributional objectives of the tax system. Writing several decades ago, economists Richard and Peggy Musgrave concluded that the distributive purposes of the tax structure in the industrialised countries had progressively weakened:

> *"Attention appears to be shifting from the traditional concern with relative income positions, with the overall state of equality, and with excessive income at the top scale, to adequacy of income at the lower end. Thus the current discussion emphasizes prevention of poverty, setting what is considered a tolerable cut-off line or floor at the lower end rather than putting a ceiling at the top, as was once a major concern."*

The tax and benefit system was still designed to reduce inequality at the 'lower end', but was no longer envisaged as a mechanism for containing the rise in inequalities at the top of the distribution. The 2008 financial crisis raised the salience of income inequality as an issue in most western societies, as acknowledged by the OECD, the International Monetary Fund (IMF), and the Governor of the Bank of England, Mark Carney. However, this trend does not appear to have been reversed over the last decade either in the United Kingdom or across the European Union, although there are still considerable differences between member-states. Short-term measures to increase taxes on high earners and the wealthy in the wake of the crash have been gradually phased out. In the meantime, there is growing concern about whether the tax and benefit system can continue to perform the limited function of constraining the growth of inequality at the lower end of the distribution, especially given the rise of absolute and relative poverty rates across the EU in recent decades.

Conclusion

Among the most influential UK analyses of tax reform in recent years has been the Mirrlees Review undertaken by the Institute for Fiscal Studies. This outlined three broad principles: the tax system ought to be integrated closely with social security and the benefits system while ensuring financial stability and resilience; it should not distort consumer behaviour, avoiding taxing economic activities differently without good reason; and it should 'achieve progressivity as efficiently as possible' by setting tax rates and allowances judiciously.

The evidence from this comparative survey is that tax and benefits systems, including in Britain, are partially achieving the final objective of 'progressivity' by promoting employment and reducing the taxation burden on labour. Nonetheless, governments across Europe are less willing to use tax rates to constrain the increase in high incomes, even in the wake of the financial crisis. In part, this reflects ongoing issues of tax resistance, as vested interests opposed to higher taxes have been able to foment growing public antipathy towards the tax state. In an era where concern about economic inequality among electorates has been rising, this raises major political challenges for social democrats in the decade ahead if the tax system is to achieve the progressive goal of constraining the increase in relative differences between the top and bottom of the income distribution.

Returning to the three broad objectives outlined by the European Commission, the UK, like other European member-states, has reformed the tax system to stabilise its public finances (although resilience remains a major concern), and to promote employment and growth in the wake of the recession. The third objective, achieving equity and fairness, appears to have been significantly downplayed. However, in a climate where popular concern about inequality is growing, this may well prove unsustainable in the long-term.

2: A HYPER-CENTRALISED ANOMALY: WHY THE UK MUST EMBRACE TAX DEVOLUTION

Tony Travers

A strange alliance of Treasury officials, social democrats and historical precedent has sustained a centralised system of taxation and spending allocation in the UK at odds with devolved structures in other countries. However, hyper-centralisation's failure to produce balanced growth across the union's different nations and regions, and the challenges posed by sub-national devolution in Scotland, suggests that it has become an anachronism. It is time the political left gave devolution a chance.

Britain has the most centralised tax-setting arrangements of any major democracy. In England, all revenues except council tax are the responsibility of the Exchequer. Until Scotland and Wales are given new tax powers, their governments will still be almost entirely funded by a block grant from the Treasury. There is a fundamental belief at the centre of British democracy that the chancellor should set all taxes and that central government should allocate resources to every sub-national institution. Indeed, the degree of centralisation suggests that Britain's national politicians have little confidence that our democracy can work effectively other than when in the hands of grandees in Westminster and Whitehall.

Even council tax is capped and frozen within both England and, under a slightly different regime, Scotland. We are in a position where the budgets of all councils are set by Whitehall. Furthermore, because the government has decided to achieve its deficit reduction policy by cutting the expenditure of a sub-set of public services, there can be no room to lessen control: council spending will have to be cut substantially further by 2019 if George Osborne's zero deficit target is to be achieved.

In fairness to the chancellor, the policy of central control over sub-national government long pre-dates his arrival at No 11. It has evolved over seven decades since the nationalisations of the immediate post-war period. As the welfare state grew, more and more of the resources to pay for it were derived from buoyant and progressive sources such as income tax. Despite efforts to widen the local tax base, notably the Layfield Committee's proposals in 1976, successive governments left the system of local property taxation largely unchanged. In 1990, Mrs Thatcher's government nationalised business rates as part of its disastrous poll tax reform. Thereafter, councils had access only to the remaining domestic property tax. It is that which has been capped and, indeed, its base has not been revalued since 1991.

Countries as diverse as Sweden, the United States, Germany, Canada, Spain and Switzerland run democratic systems which allow a dispersal of fiscal power. These nations operate successfully with taxation set at national and local levels, whether they are within 'federal' or 'unitary' arrangements. In some countries, there are three levels of tax-setting government. Germany's multi-level constitutional arrangements were put in place after 1945 and were explicitly designed to create a system of government with multiple centres of power. France achieved substantial devolution during the 1980s, while Spain has moved from being highly-centralised to a far more devolved country during the last 40 years. Britain is an outlier by any standards.

The Scots, armed with no more than ballot boxes, have forced the Treasury into an ignominious retreat over their 'total control' policy. Once Edinburgh has been given power to determine not only stamp duty but also a proportion of income tax, while also retaining a share of VAT, Scotland will have fiscal power similar to states and regions in many federal countries. Wales will follow. This will leave England as a residual, hyper-centralised, nation within the quasi-federal UK. Having said this, within Scotland and Wales, their own systems of local government are themselves relatively centralised.

How has Britain ended up with such an odd system of government and so little sub-national fiscal power? Some elements of national control can be traced back to the Fabians. Sidney and Beatrice Webb were strong proponents of centrally-imposed standards and the equalisation of resources. The refusal of George Lansbury to hand over Poplar's rates to the London County Council remains a pivotal political act, in the sense that it encouraged the introduction of grants which have had the effect of transferring resources from rich to poor areas. Even today, as a consequence of needs-equalisation grants paid to councils over many decades, spending on schools and social care tends to be highest in deprived areas.

But the decision to have inter-authority equalisation grants, which are now common in many countries, did not inevitably have to lead to centralisation of all tax-setting powers. The growth of parts of the welfare state within local government may have required centrally-funded grant support, but it did not necessarily demand the demise of local tax autonomy. What appears to have happened is that, decade after decade, Westminster and Whitehall have used a series of opportunities to justify more and more central encroachment on local power.

The Attlee government removed health and some utilities provision from local authority control in the late 1940s. Subsequently, the expanding scale of compulsory schooling, social services, housing and other 'welfare' provision required additional central grant funding. Such growth in subventions inevitably led to a 'he who pays the piper calls the tune' attitude at the centre. De-industrialisation in the 1960s and 1970s meant the government found itself under pressure to assist declining areas with new, specific, grants. Over time, these urban interventions came more and more to be streams of 'challenge' funding: councils only received the money if they spent it in ways of which Whitehall approved.

Then there was the 1980s. The rise of radical Labour councils which pushed up local taxation in opposition to the Thatcher government's policies triggered the introduction of rate-capping. In the ensuing war-of-all-against-all, there was a move from 'selective' to 'universal' capping. The Greater London Council and metropolitan county councils were abolished, removing a city-regional tier of government. The introduction of poll tax in 1990 led to the central determination of business rates. Capital spending was also subjected to a belt-and-braces control regime.

Education, much of which local government had originally developed, became politicised. As far back as 1976, James Callaghan started the process of pushing for a national system of schools in England. In a speech at Ruskin College he argued there was a "strong case for the so-called 'core curriculum' of basic knowledge ... [and] ... to maintain a proper national standard of performance ... [and an] ... inspectorate in relation to national standards". The Thatcher and Major governments then moved to school-based governance which, over time, has led to today's policy of removing local government responsibility over schools wherever possible.

Further education colleges were removed from councils during the 1990s.

So, not only was there a gradual transfer of provision away from elected local government, but its tax base was capped and eroded. While other major democracies, for example France and Spain, decentralised powers Britain did the opposite. In Spain, reform started to take place following the death of Franco in 1975, while in France the Mitterrand government decentralised power during the 1980s. In Britain the Treasury, over time, came to operate a public spending control system in which local authority activity counted pound for pound towards a national figure of 'total managed expenditure'. The 2010 decision, discussed above, to shrink the UK's budget deficit by expenditure reductions made disproportionately by local government, has created an additional justification for 100 per cent control of council budgets.

Against this unique policy background, the UK government now faces twin challenges. First, the requirement to deliver devolved fiscal power to Scotland and Wales has created pressure to 'do something' for England. Second, the commitment to reduce public expenditure to 36 per cent of GDP while ring-fencing health, pensions, schools and international development spending will create alarming consequences for the 'unprotected' services, including local government. Looking ahead, might the government find itself under pressure to devolve spending to local areas in an attempt to cope with these twin challenges?

George Osborne has been working with the ten Greater Manchester authorities on a city-regional devolution package which would give them additional powers over skills, transport, housing, planning and economic development. It is likely that the NHS will be devolved to Greater Manchester. Such reforms are, potentially, the building-blocks for wider devolution of public expenditure both to Manchester and other city regions. Legislation has been introduced to give the government powers to transfer responsibilities to groups of councils, be they in cities or counties. It is hard to know how radical this reform will turn out to be, but the growing pressures on public spending suggest there may be no option for the government but to consider a more radical package of devolution to city or county regions.

Ministers have not yet proved willing to consider fiscal devolution for England. Treasury orthodoxy holds that any form of tax differentiation will lead to competition and therefore be inefficient. However, other social democratic countries survive well with different tax levels and powers from place to place, but in Britain this is seen (particularly on the left) as risking postcode lotteries and uneven provision. There is, therefore, a strange alliance between Treasury officials and social democrats to sustain a centralised system of taxation and spending allocation.

Of course, Scotland will soon be able to set its own income tax rates, with similar powers potentially available for Wales. These radical changes will occur, we must assume, with grave misgivings among the chancellor's advisers. However, there is nothing they can do about it because Scotland has used its democratic leverage to get what it wants from the UK government.

The longer-term question of whether sub-national areas of England will be given their own, wider, tax powers depends on the future of the union. Candidates in the 2016 London mayoral contest will doubtless demand greater tax powers for the capital. Greater Manchester's leadership is also arguing for fiscal devolution. Once the Scots and the Welsh have been given their new freedoms, English councils and MPs are inevitably going to demand something more than an arcane form of England-only voting rights affecting a minority of parliamentary bills.

There is a major challenge for the Labour party in all of this. The Blair government offered the north east a minimal and under-powered form of regional government in 2004. This was rejected. There is no appetite for regional government within most of England, though the north east has latterly developed its own combined authority model of governance. City-region and county areas appear likely to be the basis of future reform in England. George Osborne has dominated national policy-making in relation to city-regions, leaving the Labour frontbench with nothing to say.

Labour leaders and mayors in cities such as Manchester, Newcastle, Liverpool, Leeds, Sheffield, Birmingham and Nottingham are closer to Osborne's mildly devolutionary view of the world than Labour's cautious centralism. Traditionally, the centre-left has taken a Fabian view about the need for equalisation, national standards and regulation. While it would not be necessary to abandon all inter-area transfers or, indeed, to remove nationally-imposed service standards, policies to devolve powers or taxation have hitherto proved hard for Labour shadow ministers to accept.

As the Labour leadership reforms itself for another five years in opposition, it will have to decide if it wants to support its own city leaders in transferring power away from Whitehall or, alternatively, attempt to slow down even the modest pace of Osborne's city-regional devolution. The failure of hyper-centralisation to produce balanced GDP per head in different nations and regions of the UK suggests that it is time to give devolution a chance. Labour could, tentatively, attempt to be radical.

3: INSTITUTIONAL INTERESTS: REVERSING THE CORPORATE TAKEOVER OF TAX POLICY

Richard Murphy

Changes in tax policy have tightened the grip of big business on tax affairs across Europe, giving undue influence to a tiny minority of tax payers. Reforms to HMRC and European institutions are needed to make tax policy better serve everyone's interests.

Tax avoidance has changed. At one time it was all about large companies making use of aggressive techniques, often involving tax havens, to reduce the amount of tax that they might pay. It was good business for those who sold tax avoidance services and most especially the bankers, lawyers and accountants engaged in this activity. Then along came the tax justice movement to spoil their show. Whether coincidentally or as a consequence, it seems likely that the large company UK corporation tax gap resulting from tax avoidance has reduced as a result. I no longer think it as high as my 2008 estimate of £12bn a year. Indeed, it may not now exceed £5bn a year.

That should be celebrated as good news. It shows that tax campaigning can work. Unfortunately, however, as one gap recedes another one is emerging into view. And it is not one that is just a consequence of sharp practice by clever corporates: it is an intended consequence of government policy. It means that I now think that the total UK large company corporate tax gap has increased even higher than it ever was, to £13bn a year. This is the consequence of the new 'corporation tax policy gap', which might be as high as £8bn a year.

This new tax gap represents the gain that large companies have made since 2008 as a result of the extensive changes in UK tax policy that they have secured. As example, the corporation tax rate for large (but not small) companies has reduced from 30 per cent to 20 per cent over that period. In addition, whilst UK multinational groups were once taxed, at least in theory, on their worldwide income, they are now only taxed in the UK on the income they have arising in this country. This is in direct contrast, for example, to the vast majority of individual UK citizens, who are still taxed on everything they earn (unless, that is, they're non-doms). This policy change has increased the appeal of tax havens to UK based multinational companies enormously. And numerous other changes, such as more generous reliefs for R&D and the tax treatment of offshore treasury functions have also greatly helped big business.

The result is that in 2015 the UK corporation tax yield (excluding North Sea revenues) will be £8bn less than forecast in 2010. Part of this may be down to growth not meeting expectations, but at least £4bn may be due to tax rate reduction, as forthcoming report for the TUC will demonstrate. Meanwhile, it is easy to allocate the rest of the shortfall to specific reliefs and allowances given based on Office for Budget Responsibility and Treasury forecasts at the time that they were introduced.

That then raises the question of how this has happened? Why is it that big business has received such an extraordinary deal since 2010 when no one else has? Could it be that this is down to HMRC governance and the way in which tax decision making is now undertaken in the UK?

When HMRC was formed in 2005, its governance arrangements were explicitly based on the interests of big business.

It was given a board that was required to have a significant number of non-executive directors, all of whom, including the chair, must be drawn from the big business community. There are about 700 companies that meet this brief in the UK at present. HMRC was, therefore, explicitly organised so that their views were not just represented, but heard loud and clear within its governance processes. The remaining 31 million direct taxpayers in the UK were, in contrast, denied a voice.

We have, as a result, reached the absurd situation where the current chair of HMRC is a former senior tax partner in KPMG, a firm whose US branch was fined $456 million for criminal tax abuse in the USA as recently as 2005. Also on the board is a former CEO of Npower, who happened to be director of that group's Maltese subsidiaries which used to route interest payments from the UK to Germany in a manner designed to save tens if not hundreds of millions of pounds in tax. Furthermore, over recent years people associated with PWC, Tesco and Barclays have also served. It would be hard to make up such an arrangement of poachers turned gamekeepers. Many of the large companies accused of tax avoidance in the UK, and those who advise them, now have extraordinary institutional influence over the UK's tax authority, whose prime task is *meant* to be challenging the arrangements those very same companies create.

This is not the only area where large businesses have been afforded undue influence in the tax law making process due to reforms that superficially appear to be about making it more accountable. The consultation processes now regularly undertaken with regard to proposed tax reforms and draft legislation are another area where a process that appears to have democratic intent has actually been captured by big business and its representatives. They can do this because only they can afford the time and effort, and sometimes only they have the spare specific expertise required, to engage in these consultation processes.

A similar story can be told of many of the committees at the OECD, where business representatives have dominated all consultation hearings on, for example, the Base Erosion and Profit Shifting project that is intended to tackle tax avoidance. This is because few others have the time and resources to send people to take part in this process.

The situation is slightly different in the EU, but the effect is the same, with many tax and accounting consultations also dominated by the voices of these companies and accounting firms. Accounting provides the best example here (partly because much of tax law is devolved to member states). In 2001 the European Commission encouraged the creation of EFRAG – the European Financial Reporting Advisory Group. Its task was to advise on the development of accounting standards, an issue that now has significant crossover with tax issues on such matters as country-by-country reporting. The advisory group is, however, made up entirely of accounting, banking and insurance groups: civil society is not represented at all.

The consequences of such selective consultation in the UK are clear. HMRC, as a non-ministerial UK department, has ended up with an unusual range of permanent secretaries. Some have been over-dominant, appearing to have been accepted as policy makers in the absence of ministerial guidance. Meanwhile, others appear to serve the interests of tax abusers, enabling tax evaders to use a tax saving disclosure scheme that they were previously excluded from using. The overall result is that massively undue influence has been given to a tiny minority of taxpayers in the whole tax setting process. That it is these taxpayers that have unduly benefitted, wittingly or unwittingly, as a result of enormous tax cuts that no other group in society has enjoyed is the almost inevitable outcome.

The question is, then, what can be done about this? I have four suggestions.

The first is to appoint a cabinet-level minister to be responsible for HMRC who would be answerable for it in both parliament and to other departments and agencies. This need not in any way breach taxpayer confidentiality, but is essential for accountability on such a key political issue. At present, as a non-ministerial department, HMRC frequently does not take part in inter-departmental discussions related to relevant policy making, which it has a clear interest in. We need to sweep away the historical anachronism of the current unaccountable situation that dates back to the ancient disputes between crown and parliament, and which should have been left behind in the civil war era.

Second, HMRC needs to be subject to more rigorous and independent review than has been provided by the National Audit Office. When that Office went to exceptional lengths to try to deny the supply of information to the Public Accounts Committee during the last parliament it proved itself unfit to be the agent of our elected representatives seeking to hold HMRC to account. What we need instead is an Office for Tax Responsibility, well-funded and well-staffed, accountable to either the Treasury or Public Accounts Committee (or maybe both, in joint session, rather like the joint defence committee arrangements). As Margaret Hodge has proved, it is for our politicians to hold HMRC to account, but they need the resources to do so and such an Office for Tax Responsibility could provide that. If it were also to review all tax policy proposals and associated forecasts independently of HMRC and the Treasury parliamentary debate on these issues would be vastly better informed.

Third, the tax consultations and committees that meet on a regular basis with HMRC and represent the views of taxpayers are important. However, it is for this reason that public funding should be supplied to ensure that those who have opinions that need to be heard can be truly engaged in these processes. Any group seeking to make representation should be able to bid for funding to cover the reasonable costs of making submissions to HMRC during a consultation process, such as hiring expert opinion and costs incurred in attending hearings. Only then will ordinary taxpayers, small businesses, pensioners, charities and others be truly represented in these processes.

And last, HMRC board appointments should be subject to a quota system so that it is ensured that a wide range of taxpayer interests are represented on that board. After all, management experience is not limited to big business and as HMRC has to engage with society in all its manifestations it is vital that its Board represents those various interests.

The same lessons need to be learned elsewhere. It is absurd that neither the OECD nor EU will fund representations from those stakeholders from whom they seek engagement (including those from developing countries in the case of the OECD), and instead demand that those wishing to make representations must be self-funded. The resulting processes are inevitably biased and unrepresentative as a consequence. Relatively modest sums expended on the reasonable costs incurred of those making representations could ensure that consultations were open and balanced.

Tax is too important to be left to very narrow interests, but that is what has happened in the UK and worldwide over the last few years. It is high time that this was changed, and now is the time to begin the process. These suggestions would take us a long way in the right direction.

4: GLOBAL TAX AVOIDANCE: HAS THE FIGHT ONLY JUST BEGUN?

Faiza Shaheen and Beck Smith

Tax avoidance is higher on the global political agenda than it ever has been before, largely as a result of civil society's hard work. However, we have a long way to go to include developing countries, increase transparency and tackle tax havens. Furthermore, we need to make a positive case for paying tax to halt a global race to the bottom on rates.

Tax avoidance is probably not the most obvious candidate for dinner party conversation but, as every tax justice campaigner knows, there is far more to the topic than technical terms and boring men in suits. Global tax avoidance is a story of multinational companies getting one over on developing and developed countries alike; the nefarious schemes of a greedy rich elite; and even corrupt politicians and arms dealers hiding ill-gotten gains. Believe it or not, global tax avoidance is more of a bestselling mystery thriller novel than a school textbook.

Recently, the plot has thickened. It has become increasingly obvious that this is not simply a David and Goliath story about big business or rich individuals and the public: it is also about rich states versus poor, and between the citizen and government. As such we have reached a critical juncture in the tax story and the next encounter could be the bloodiest yet.

Politicians across Europe have clearly changed gears on the issue of tax avoidance, from nonchalance to strong rhetoric and real action. However, alongside celebrating successes we need to admit four oversights which include: developing countries being left out of the decision-making process; limited public access to new beneficial ownership registries, which state exactly who the owner of a company is; insufficient clamp down on crown dependencies and overseas territories (better known as tax havens); and, failing to make the positive case for tax more generally, allowing 'a race to the bottom' on corporate taxes.

Below we take stock of progress and consider these four challenges as we prepare for the next stage in the battle for global tax justice.

Where are we in the journey towards tax justice?

We cannot overstate the importance of civil society in getting us to this point. The issue of tax avoidance has been championed by think tanks and civil society organisations at the highest levels for the past decade. Reports such as Christian Aid's *Hidden Profits: The EU's role in supporting an unjust global tax system* have highlighted the EU's role in implicitly almost institutionalising tax avoidance and how, in an ever-globalised world, the issue increasingly transcends actions within national borders. This work, alongside media attraction to scandal and WikiLeaks revelations, has led to a public outcry forcing governments to take action.

As tax justice has moved up the political agenda we have seen countries taking both unilateral and multilateral action. The OECD has played a leading role and its Global Forum is a place where countries can work together to increase tax transparency. One of the most important things it has done is to look at the information that countries exchange about tax in order to help governments enforce their own domestic tax laws. However, there are clear biases in the work of the OECD towards rich countries, a point we will address in the next section.

A clear high point in the tax justice timeline was when the UK government used its recent presidency of the G8 in 2013 to focus on ensuring tax compliance and promoting greater tax transparency. This championing of tax justice firmly placed it on the G8/7 and the G20 agenda for the longer term.

Another milestone was the recent announcement of a European tax transparency package. This package of measures demonstrates the commitment to tax justice at EU level. Their plans to introduce the automatic exchange of information between member states on their tax rulings are both welcome and feasible and will encourage greater country co-ordination.

Overall, we can conclude that it hasn't been a case of 'all talk and no action.' New policies have been introduced and there is increasing recognition that tax is not purely an issue of national sovereignty but a policy area with significant repercussions beyond country borders. However, the preceding era of action on tax justice is equivalent to picking the low hanging fruit. The next era will require structural shifts in global politics and the matching of rhetoric with action. In a world overly influenced by fat cats and their lobbyists, this will not be easy.

The importance of developing countries in the tax debate

Functioning tax systems are the cornerstone of democracies, of tackling inequality and of supporting crucial public services. This rationale for the creation of robust tax systems is even more relevant in developing countries where there is a lack of access to essential public services and poor government accountability. But raising taxes in developing countries is not just a matter of national action. Developing countries lose out from tax avoidance disproportionately, in particular via illicit financial flows. These parts of the tax agenda must be tackled globally.

According to the African Union/Economic Commission for Africa *High Level Panel on Illicit Financial Flows from Africa* report, the continent lost about $1tn between 1980 and 2008. Save the Children's own *Making a Killing* report found that $15bn is lost in tax revenue from trade mis-invoicing in Sub-Saharan Africa alone. Once you convert these figures into lost health inputs, the human costs of this avoidance become even more apparent: in Kenya the tax losses were more than the average health spend between 2002 and 2010. While the exact estimations are difficult to decipher, what cannot be denied is that huge sums of money are lost from developing countries with dire consequences for economic growth and human development.

While harmonisation and co-operation at an EU or OECD has indicated progress on tax avoidance, they have represented to many an exclusive club of action. The OECD's ongoing Base Erosion and Profit Shifting (BEPS) project has received criticism from many NGOs as a result of the inclusion of developing countries in discussions seemingly coming as an afterthought instead of making sure they had a seat at the table from the start. Global problems cannot be fixed with regional solutions.

For the past six months the NGO community and major developing countries have been involved in a bitter battle with rich countries to open up the decision making process. But, at the time of writing, it looks unlikely that new global tax norms setting body will be established at the Financing for Development discussions in Addis Ababa in July 2015.

Making it public

Making tax records open to the public may seem like a subsidiary point but it is fundamental to ensuring on-going tax justice and achieving the aim of increasing tax transparency. We need to know who owns companies, where those companies are based, how much profit those companies make, how much tax they're paying and crucially, where in the world they're paying tax.

The current draft of the Addis Ababa Action Agenda fails to highlight the need for public reporting. Without this public scrutiny it is much easier for bad behaviour to go under the radar.

Tax havens

The issue of tax havens is critical to tax justice. It is estimated that assets hidden in tax havens may represent a loss to the public revenues of developing countries of between $120-160bn a year. While too many rich countries refuse to even publically admit that tax havens exist, the UK at least had some strong rhetoric on tax havens. However, the current Conservative government has chosen to take a 'softly softly' approach rather than threatening to penalise tax havens for non-compliance. This has resulted in considerable feet dragging across tax havens with many of the crown dependencies and overseas territories choosing to undertake drawn out consultation processes on increased transparency which just lead back to business as usual.

More generally we have failed to make tax avoidance not worth doing. For example, the recent tax evasion scandal involving HSBC's Swiss subsidiary has seen only one person prosecuted despite there being more than 1,000 account holders. Such little punishment clearly sends the wrong signal.

Missing the point: making the positive case for tax

The OECD found that corporate taxes have seen a pronounced shift downwards across high-income countries and developing countries have also engaged in a race-to-the-bottom on corporate tax, too often prompted by multinational companies threatening to go elsewhere if not given beneficial tax rates. Worse still, tax subsidies in cash starved developing countries are not uncommon. One can only conclude that while we have been winning the argument on tax collection, we have been losing the argument on tax.

The reality is that people don't always get why they should be paying tax and corporates do not always recognise their moral responsibility. Somewhere in the midst of technical terms and minutiae policy details we have forgotten to remind everyone that tax is what pays for vital and beloved health services, educating our children and building our roads. Private finance cannot replace public finance to deliver essential services.

Where next?

What the journey so far on tax justice has shown is that change is possible. It is also clear that we are nowhere near the finish line. We need to significantly shift the dial on issues such as inclusiveness and tax havens or risk stagnation or even undoing the good work that has been done. We must continue to make the moral case and we may also need to get more technical to be able to understand the detail and ensure we are really getting progress on tax.

After a long battle, the need to tackle tax avoidance is finally at the forefront of the minds of politicians and the public alike. We must continue to fight hard to keep it there.

5: SOMETHING FOR SOMETHING: REMAKING THE CASE FOR HYPOTHECATED TAXATION

Andrew Harrop

In the context of constrained public finances, developing a clearer link between taxes paid and revenue spent is more important than ever. Significant new spending in areas such as health and social care should be funded through earmarked tax rises. The UK also has an unexpected opportunity to revive National Insurance and should consider turning it into a fully ring-fenced fund, along the lines of continental social insurance schemes.

It is 15 years since the Fabian Society's Commission on Taxation and Citizenship proposed that hypothecation should play a central part in UK revenue raising. The commissioners called for earmarked tax rises to be linked to improvements in public services – paving the way for Gordon Brown's now famous increase in National Insurance to fund the NHS. Indeed, in 2000, the majority of the commissioners wanted to go even further and ringfence a proportion of income tax as a dedicated NHS tax.

In the years that have followed, neither Labour nor the coalition fully embraced the principle of hypothecation, but both have used it in practice. George Osborne's summer budget was a case in point, with the chancellor reviving the concept of a hypothecated road fund, something last seen in the 1930s. The weakest version of hypothecation – the idea of earmarking new or increased taxes to particular public spending commitments – is now a standard tool for introducing revenue-neutral reforms. It sits alongside ideas like 'switch spend' and 'tax swaps' (which substitute one area of spending or taxation for another) in an era of tight public finances.

Earmarking is especially important for parties in opposition, which need to prove economic credibility by showing that their sums add up. In 2015 Labour, the Liberal Democrats and UKIP (but not the SNP) all unveiled manifestos which they claimed to be fully costed. Labour's programme included tax rises on bankers' bonuses, hedge funds and expensive homes, each linked to specific public service commitments.

Meanwhile, for the Conservatives, earmarking is not only important in order to prevent any new commitment from undermining the party's broader austerity narrative, it is also a way to signal fairness. For example, when the coalition government decided to support the 'Dilnot' social care funding reforms (which benefit better off pensioners by capping the extent to which assets need to be run down to pay for care), the chancellor announced they would be part funded by a freezing of inheritance tax thresholds.

Taxation purists have always argued that earmarking is a political deception, because the public can never know the counterfactual of what would have happened without the tax rise. However, the 2002 increase in national insurance shows that this soft form of hypothecation need not be a fiscal fiction. It was followed by a significant and sustained increase in health spending which there has been no political appetite to reverse; this illustrates that, since public spending is often 'path dependent', the influence of past earmarked tax rises can endure.

Having said that, earmarking is a fraught business in the context of deficit reduction, because it artificially detaches particular decisions from the wider context of spending restraint and/or higher taxation. For example, the 'new money' linked to the Dilnot reforms is significantly less than the real spending cuts that adult social care will experience as a consequence of austerity.

But if you look beyond the immediate cuts, the strategic case for earmarking grows stronger. This is because we are entering a period where there will be a broad political consensus against running a structural deficit but also strong upward pressures on expenditure. As a result, after austerity, politicians may need to make the case for more spending and more taxes to pay for it. If this is the case, earmarking will matter for securing public understanding and consent. Moreover, in this context, any new spending is unlikely to benefit everyone evenly: where one group of people are particular beneficiaries (or are 'under-paying' at present), using earmarking will allow new taxes to be targeted especially towards them.

These conditions particularly apply in the case of health and social care, where there is an emerging consensus that funding needs are rising relative to GDP.[1] This upward pressure means that, unless the overall tax burden is increased, health-related spending will 'crowd-out' spending for the future, on children, skills and capital investment. Earmarked tax rises will help communicate this dilemma and convince the public.

There is also a powerful case for asking the first beneficiaries of new health and care spending – the current cohort of older people – to make a particular contribution. This is because, after the economic crisis, the typical pensioner household now has, not only more assets, but also a higher standard of living than the median pre-retirement household.[2] This is partly because pensioners pay less in tax each year than working-age families with the same income and family size, as the Fabian Society report *A Presumption of Equality* described. Moreover, the National Institute for

Economic and Social Research forecasts that today's older cohorts (unlike younger adults) will pay less in taxes than they will receive in state support over the course of their lives. As a result, proposing a 'something for something' deal for older people seems both fairer and more politically acceptable than increasing taxes across the board.

So we have seen that, since 2000 the earmarking of tax increases has become commonplace and that there are good reasons for it to continue. By contrast, fuller forms of hypothecation have largely been ignored and rarely feature in debates on future revenue raising (unless you count the devolution of tax-raising powers to Scotland). Indeed, in some respects things have moved backwards, with the political parties further blurring the lines between taxation and national insurance (which is officially hypothecated). For example, Alistair Darling raised national insurance to tackle the deficit, not to fund contributory entitlements; and the coalition then offset this measure with cuts in income tax – in effect, a stealthy tax swap.

In the UK, the idea behind national insurance is out of fashion. It is an example of European-style social insurance, characterised by hypothecated contributions, significant risk-pooling and cross-subsidies among members. This concept has been ignored in recent years, when social provision has been expanded. Instead entitlements have either been funded by general taxation or by new contribution requirements which have taken a highly individualised form. For example, student finance and workplace pensions are each regulated and heavily subsidised by government, but they involve 'personal accounts' not shared funds.

We have forgotten that on the continent people often think of three tiers of social support: at one end, basic entitlements funded by taxation; at the other, individualised entitlements, directly associated with personal payments; but also, in between, social insurance funded by ringfenced but pooled contributions. Yet curiously, while this taxonomy is unfamiliar in the UK debate, it is a good description of the emerging UK pension system – as long as national insurance is still thought of as a hypothecated insurance scheme. Once the current pension reforms are all in place we will have a small tax-funded safety net; heavily regulated and subsidised, account-based private pensions; and, in the middle, a good, flat-rate state pension, funded and earned through social insurance contributions.

As a result, and almost by accident, the UK has created the conditions for a revival in the national insurance principle – if we wish to grasp it. National insurance can, for the first time in decades, be presented as a fair 'contract', where national insurance contributions (NICs) buy people something they have real reason to value: a decent, earnings-linked state pension. And with the rise in the value and cost of national insurance benefits, contributions into the national insurance fund now broadly match payments out. This means that it would be possible to establish national insurance as a properly independent system, along continental lines. For example, last year the IPPR floated the idea of ending Treasury top-ups to the national insurance fund (which would establish full hypothecation, with contributions matching receipts) and establishing it as a visible, autonomous institution.

Balancing arrangements would be needed to account for the ebb and flow of contributions and working-age claims, across the economic cycle. But, nevertheless, this proposal has the attraction of transparency and would create a greater sense of contribution, responsibility and ownership with respect to social entitlements. People would feel that they had earned the benefits funded from national insurance –

and this might help counter the negativity associated with social security more broadly.

There are also good financial reasons for considering an independent fund. Over the coming decades the cost of the state pension will rise, relative to GDP, so from the perspective of the public finances, a ring-fenced fund might help to prevent other valuable spending from being crowded-out. And, if and when increases in NICs appeared necessary in order to fund pensions, the public would have a direct stake in the trade-offs between price and generosity.

Similarly, the complete ringfencing of national insurance would create the opportunity to debate the costs and benefits of better working-age protection. For example, there is a case for paying (time-limited) job seekers' allowance, employment and support allowance and maternity allowance at the same rate as the state pension, in exchange for slightly higher NICs. This would address an existing market failure and create another 'contract', where contribution would earn people entitlements worth valuing. With a ring-fenced fund it would become possible to have this discussion without it feeling like a zero-sum trade-off between earned entitlements and (more progressive) means-tested benefits. Instead, it would be possible to weigh up the best way to give typical workers decent protection from loss of earnings, by rationally evaluating the option of social insurance against a 'personal account'-style solution involving funded insurance schemes.

Creating a truly ringfenced, hypothecated system of national insurance is entirely feasible over the course of a parliament. It would be a rare opportunity to change course, in a field of public policy which is usually bedevilled by path dependency. The question is whether this shift to a continental model would be too much of a departure from the dominance of Treasury centralism. But (as with the debate on localism) it is at least time to debate whether our politics can cope with some pluralism in the way we raise revenue and determine entitlements.

If politicians do nothing then national insurance really does not have a future. In which case, policy makers should stop pretending NICs are different and gradually absorb them into income tax. This has the benefit of simplicity. It could also make personal taxation more progressive and inter-generationally balanced (since unearned incomes and pensions are not subject to national insurance). But, set alongside the withering of contributory social security before retirement, it would be a decisive retreat from Beveridge's famous declaration: "benefit in return for contributions, rather than free allowances from the state, is what the people of Britain desire".

Notes

1. Barker, K et al, *A new settlement for health and social care,* King's Fund, 2014; Charlesworth, A, *NHS finances: the challenges all political parties need to face,* Health Foundation, 2015.
2. Households Below Average Income: 1994/95 to 1013/14, Department for Work and Pensions, 2015.

National insurance: a case study

National insurance (NI) is a system of insurance for times when earnings are interrupted or cease altogether. The main contingency provided for, in terms of length of time and amount of expenditure, is retirement, though maternity, sickness and unemployment are also covered. But, crucially, this is *social* insurance, in which the match between what is paid in and paid out (contributions and benefits) does not have to be exact, and does not necessarily have to relate to differential risk profiles. So society as a whole can decide how inclusive the system is, and how closely it mirrors the reality of risks experienced by different groups.

This is very different from private insurance. Social insurance can cover a wider range of risks and risk groups. It is also possible to vary the amount of earnings covered; the way in which part-time or self-employed workers are treated; the amount of contributions required; and any ceiling on the amount of benefits received. If the NI system did not exist, those who could afford it would still probably have insurance (and other arrangements) to cover personal risks; but such insurance would be private, meaning the *social* – and hence potentially risk sharing, redistributive and more inclusive – element of coverage would be removed.

Most social security systems have a social insurance component. Those countries in which the social partners (employers and unions) have a role in managing the system – as in France and Germany, for example – are less likely to see social security contributions as a form of taxation. Social insurance recognises contribution in the form of paid work, and in some cases caring responsibilities; encourages formal employment; and means that employers do not have to meet all their employees' needs. Social insurance benefits are not means-tested, and so do not depend on the presence, resources or activities of a claimant's partner. They provide independent income for individuals in couples, and are therefore important for preserving autonomy, particularly important for women. They can also act to prevent poverty, rather than relieving it after the event as means-tested benefits attempt (often rather unsuccessfully) to do.

However, the chancellor has proposed to increase the personal tax allowance significantly in real terms, and indeed has already done so over the past few years, whilst the NI contributions threshold has not been increased in the same way. So a backlash is possible from low-paid workers in particular, as they find themselves no longer liable for income tax but still paying NI contributions.

This would be problematic, in part because this example of hypothecation does appear to work. Increases in NI contributions over recent years seem to have been generally accepted by the public, whereas any tax increases have been highly controversial. People do seem to feel they have 'paid for' NI benefits (and the NHS, which is funded to a small extent from NI contributions too), and therefore have some sense of ownership. See, for example, research cited in the Fabian Society's Commission on Taxation and Citizenship report *Paying for Progress.*

But the real terms reductions in working age NI benefits, combined with restrictions in entitlement, have arguably led to a growing feeling of public insecurity (see, for example, Michael Orton's Compass report

Something's Not Right) and a related sense that the 'undeserving' – those who are seen as not having contributed – do better out of the system than those who have. This has been described by Kate Bell and Declan Gaffney as a 'nothing for something' problem (rather than the 'something for nothing' issue so popular amongst some politicians and media). Younger people in particular have much lower expectations of state provision in the future, as Demos research has shown.

Realistically, a merger of NI contributions and income tax is highly unlikely, even though it is sometimes mooted, because this would result in income tax rates increasing. Indeed, the current government is proposing legislation to prevent increases in income tax (and NI contributions) rates. It therefore looks as though NI contributions are here to stay. If this is the case, we need a rejuvenated, modernised social insurance system of NI benefits, suited to today's flexible labour market and fluid families, and recognising different forms of contribution to society. In addition, we need imaginative ways of increasing the sense of public ownership that has been attenuated over the years of cutbacks and more restrictive rules of entitlement.

Fran Bennett

6: ON THE MARGINS: TACKLING GENDER BIAS IN THE TAX SYSTEM

Ann Mumford

Every aspect of a tax system has the potential to affect the position of women detrimentally. The challenge of a coherent, revised tax policy, informed by the important development of gender budgeting, would be to move women from the margin, into the economic mainstream.

The problem of women's comparative poverty with men cannot be solved by the taxation system on its own. However, it very frequently provides the forum for efforts by governments to deal with the basic, intransigent fact of women's poverty. These efforts are not misguided but important, in large part because of the discussion that they enable. But tax needs to be part of wider changes in the socio-economy.

Although tax may be incapable of truly addressing women's economic inequality, there are sound choices that can be made to reduce gender bias in tax systems. Individual filing of tax returns for earnings and investment income, as opposed to joint filing for married couples, has been available in the UK since 1990 and is a good illustration of such a choice. Additionally, the decision of the (then) Inland Revenue in the 1970s to stop corresponding only with husbands on tax matters is another example of an important and good change. When explicit bias is revealed in tax systems, it is important to redress it.

The effort required to redress it, however, should not be underestimated. For example, individual filing is a highly contested issue in Germany and one that seems unlikely to be resolved any time soon. The fear is that, if it were introduced, then families as a unit would pay more tax. Thus, the ideology and the symbolism are heavily charged. Similarly, the classification of women's sanitary products as luxury items for VAT purposes, for reasons of ideology, is increasingly dominating discussion of tax and gender.

This, however, is a diversion from discussion of truly radical reform in the UK, which involves asking an important and difficult question: how does tax contribute to gender bias in ownership of capital? Generally, questions of 'explicit bias' are easier to remedy than questions of 'implicit bias', which necessarily involve subjective judgments about appropriate economic behaviour. Although analyses of questions of implicit bias may be difficult, within tax law in particular, the potential of their analysis is particularly rich. Gender budgeting is illustrative in this context, as it presents a sturdy point from which to begin the search for implicit bias. Indeed, the fact of gender budgeting establishes that there is a *presumption* of gender bias in fiscal budgetary processes, which starts the discussion.

HM Treasury has committed to using gender budgeting – interrogations of budgets to determine allocation of money along gender lines – as part of its standard consultation procedure. The aim is to identify a number of things, including any disconnect between policy goals and resources promised to support them; or, any underappreciated or unrealised impact upon women's poverty. The fundamental starting point, which has particular resonance given the continued influence of Thomas Piketty's *Capital* on how we view distribution of wealth, would be to recognise that where tax breaks for capital are offered, these breaks are likely to be subsidised by those who possess the least. So, for example, tax breaks for double taxation of dividends is typically viewed in terms of the impact upon the perception of the UK as a locus for international investment. It is not typically considered from the perspective of the dominant gender of shareholders.

The link between gender budgeting and the tax system lies in the significance of the budget itself. There is an initial, obvious link, in that if taxes were not collected, then it would be difficult to finance a budget. If governments have established gender budgeting to account for discrepancies in spending according to gender, then it is possible that these discrepancies extend to the tax system. The budget is not just about spending money; it is also about choosing a way in which an economy might be organised. The way to pressure policymakers to care about the results of gender budgeting is by fostering recognition that it indeed is possible for a society to choose the economy it wants. There is nothing inevitable about women's economic inequality. Tax policies are never gender neutral – they always represent a choice. Women and men will benefit from a market economy based on gender fairness. It is possible to have this discussion, and to make it a policy goal.

Every aspect of a tax system has the potential to affect women. A chapter which analyses every aspect of the tax system, and attendant case law, and then attempts to forge a bridge back to a theory of women, tax and the law may risk finding that the bridge is unable to bear the weight of the analyses. Thus, it is necessary to explain the arguments which follow. Some aspects of tax law in other countries may serve to redistribute more money to more women than occurs in the UK. For example, the Swedish welfare state is frequently hailed as approximating the closest version of meaningful state support and therefore encouragement for the dual-earner, dual-carer family, sharing burdens more equally between genders. However, it is important to note that women's poverty persists as a global problem. It is universal, but not homogenous. What works well in another country may not work as well in the UK.

Women are more likely to be poor, and the tax system is part of the problem. One approach to this chapter would be to suggest that the status of women within the economy is best analysed by addressing the question of money. If women disproportionately live in poverty, for example, then their status is clear, and it is patently not a good one. Put differently, it should not be difficult to identify exactly which provisions of tax law benefit women: rather, it is necessary to choose those laws which give women, as an interest group, the most money. However, sometimes a government initiative which is clearly about redistribution, such as the benefits system, may be difficult to administer effectively in the face of a competing goal.

For example, most political parties endeavour to be viewed as supportive of the family unit. Given that tax is one of the most important tools that a government has for affecting the economy, it is to be expected that the tax system would be used by a government to promote the impression that it does, indeed, support the family. The family is however an uncertain locus for the promotion of gender equality objectives. It is difficult to locate fiscal justice, or indeed tax policy generally, within the family unit.

What, exactly, is tax policy? There are different ways in which this question might be addressed. Tax policy, for example, could be identified as the goals which tax legislation is structured to achieve. Given that Boyd and Young have warned that, "when it comes to tax policy decisions, feminists still have little influence",[1] it might be assumed that what is necessary is for women to identify equality goals, and then to lobby for legislation which supports them.

Yet there may be competing goals. In the face of this, it will be necessary for governments to make choices. Young observed that it is the "invisibility of the inequalities" suffered by women through tax law that is most troubling, and it is with this aspect of the nature of implicit bias that this chapter hopes to engage. For example, to what extent does taxation of the family unit support a market economy which largely undervalues unpaid labour, if it values it at all?

Additionally, why should taxes bridge this divide? Put simply, taxes are useful. Taxes help us to think about which activities in a socio-economy should contribute to the funding of the state, and which should be supported by the state. Taxes also enable discussion between government and taxpayers. To illustrate, whether or not green taxes ultimately achieve a significant impact upon efforts to contain global warming, the fact of their existence communicates to taxpayers the value that governments place on 'green' choices. This argument also applies to taxes which aim to encourage, or discourage, some behaviours. Whether or not the cost of a packet of cigarettes ultimately discourages smokers, the fact of its cost (if perceived to be inflated by taxes) communicates disapproval. The challenge is to spend sufficient time and care considering the message that is being communicated. If an increase in the tax on cigarettes is likely to impact the poorest most severely, and if women are more likely than men to be poor, then an increase in the cost of cigarettes may contribute to the poverty of women in the UK. If this contribution goes unnoticed, if it is subsumed within the general (presumed gender neutral) discussion of 'sin taxes,' then what message is communicated about the status of women?

The goal should be to prioritise the issue of women's economic inequality. If every tax policy initiative were interrogated with the single question – "even if this initiative is laudable and valuable (for example, if its intention is to discourage people from smoking), will it nonetheless exacerbate women's poverty?" – the outcome could be significant. It need not follow that the tax policy initiative in question will fail as an outcome, but it may follow that women's poverty will be more visible.

On a broader scale, there may well be a strong argument for forging a global tax policy, perhaps along the lines of the radical reconsideration of redistribution of wealth suggested by Piketty. Where capital grows in value more quickly than income, and with such striking historical patterns, it may be time to consider deploying the tax system for the pragmatic solutions at which Piketty hints. The Office for National Statistics has released figures demonstrating that taxes and benefits have the greatest impact on income being shared more equally between households. Put differently, taxes are the most important tool for the redistribution of wealth that Piketty's research suggests may be necessary. The UK could seek to lead this discussion.

There are still many aspects of the relationship between taxpayer and the state that render tax law, as a subject, domestic. Indeed in some ways, tax could be described as an intensely personal relationship, insofar as the relationship between taxpayer and the state is concerned. One of the reasons for this is the great secret of tax law: if every taxpayer in the UK were to decide to stop paying taxes, then it would make little sense for the government to try to force them. It would cost too much to enforce a tax system in which every taxpayer has embraced noncompliance. Thus – and it is perhaps this thought which lends the most power to tax – taxes in a sense are voluntary, or at the least a part of a fragile and significant agreement between taxpayers and state.

Within a UK context, it should be possible to address questions of tax and inequality from the perspective of gender. First, the Women's Budget Group have demonstrated consistently that the single greatest change to the tax system that would enhance women's economic equality is a renewed focus on raising greater tax revenue. Taxes may be deployed in a number of ways, as they have argued, that may assist women. Secondly, it is also important to resist changes that will reduce women's economic autonomy and independence. The option within the (delayed) Universal Credit to ask one member of a family to receive the credit carries with it a number of risks for women's financial autonomy; most pressingly, as the WBG have argued, it appears to support the 'single breadwinner' model.

Within a global context, tax and inequality are currently understood on a transnational scale, and as part of global movements, in a manner which is perhaps historically unprecedented. Incorporating the question of women and economic inequality within these movements carries striking potential. The OECD (with its Base Erosion and Profit Shifting project) and the UN (with its Committee of Experts on International Cooperation in Tax Matters and other initiatives), have demonstrated that they are devoting attention and resources to questions of tax enforcement and, crucially, tax policy. There is ample scope for incorporating questions of women, tax and economic inequality. The problem of women's economic inequality is universal, and cannot be solved by tax law, in any state, or through any tax-based international agreement. Tax law is not a capable forum for redressing gender equality. And it is difficult to identify precisely which provisions of tax law benefit women, because every aspect of a tax system has the potential to affect women. Ultimately, tax systems put women on the margin. The challenge of a coherent, revised tax policy, informed by the important development of gender budgeting, would be to move women from the margin, into the economic mainstream.

Notes

1. S. B. Boyd & C. F. L. Young, 'Feminism, Law, and Public Policy: Family Feuds and Taxing Times', (2004) 42 *Osgoode Hall Law Journal* 545–582, at p.580. The were writing about Canada, although this statement appears to this author to be universal in application.

7: A WEALTH OF OPTIONS: SHIFTING TAX AWAY FROM EARNED INCOMES

Howard Glennerster

Inequalities in wealth are far greater than inequalities in income on which most tax policy discussion has focused. However, different kinds of wealth require different kinds of taxation, and there are a range of potential policy options we can consider, from a site value tax on property to a local income tax to replace regressive council tax. Each option faces obstacles, but each provide the opportunity for a fairer society and more efficient economy, in the interests of everyone.

A powerful case can be made for shifting the weight of taxation from earned income to wealth, such as property, land and financial assets. This case rests not just on claims of fairness but on economic efficiency. Taxing work but not taxing rising property values creates perverse incentives to invest in property not work. And letting private owners reap most of the rewards of public infrastructure investment restricts the optimal scale of major projects. Ultimately, the whole economy loses.

But fairness matters. Inequalities in wealth are far greater than inequalities in income on which most tax policy discussion has focused. Those on the cusp of being in the top 10 per cent of incomes receive four times the income of those in the equivalent bottom tenth position: for wealth that figure is 70 times. Furthermore, in the years between 2010 and 2012, one in ten households had less than £15,000 of savings or assets, while the top one per cent had on average £1.2 million.[1]

There are significant consequences for such inequitable wealth distribution. Young adults brought up in families lacking savings suffer in later life. Not to possess any assets minimises families' capacity to plan ahead and take risks, change career and train, or move house to find work. And the extreme wealth of a few can pervert the political process via influential vested interests.

These are not arguments that should resonate only with a few lefty socialists. They should matter to all who care about creating an open and efficient society. Yet European governments' record on taxing wealth has been lamentable. In the post war period, UK taxes on inheritance amounted to 1.5 per cent of GDP. This has fallen to about 0.2 per cent today. Taxes on net wealth, property, inheritance and gifts amount to just over 4 per cent of national income but less than 1 per cent of total national wealth. Moreover, most of that revenue comes from council tax which is levied in a regressive way on renting residents, not home owners.

In the OECD as a whole, taxes on assets, property and inheritances amount to only 2 per cent of GDP each year, as Table 1 shows. Nowhere are taxes on wealth of much revenue significance.

Yet wealth has been growing faster than incomes in most countries as well as becoming more concentrated. In France and England, for example, the sum total of their wealth was equivalent to three times their GDP in 1980 and five times in 2009. What exactly constitutes 'total wealth' differs somewhat in different countries, as the last column in Table 2 demonstrates, but the general trend is clear.

Table 1: Taxes on assets as a percentage of GDP 2013

	Recurrent net wealth	Property	Inheritance, gift	Total asset taxes
France	0.2	3.8	0.5	4.5
Germany	0	0.9	0.2	1.1
Italy	0.2	2.7	0	2.9
Netherlands	0	1.1	0.2	1.3
Sweden	0	1.1	-	1.1
UK	0	4.1	0.1	4.3
OECD	0.2	1.8	0.1	2.1

OECD Revenue Statistics: Comparative Tables stats.oecd.org (accessed 21 June 2015)

Table 2: Growth wealth holdings compared to incomes

	Period	Wealth to income ratio	Measure of ratios
France	1980–2009	From 3 to 5:1	Total private
Germany	1978–2003	From 3 to 3.5:1	Total
Italy	1987–2006	From 4.5 to 6.5:1	Total median household
Netherlands	1993–2011	From 2.9 to 4.7:1	Mean household
Sweden	1978–1992 2002–2004	From 3.6 to 2:1 From 2.7 to 3:1	Total
UK	1980–2005	From 3 to 5:1	Personal wealth to GDP

V. Maestri, F. Bogliacino and W. Salverda 2014,[2] for UK J.Hills and F. Bastagli 2015[3]

Even so several countries have abandoned taxing annual net wealth (Sweden, Netherlands, Germany and Finland), and/or have reduced taxes on inheritances.

Difficulties in regularly assessing wealth holdings, for fear that such taxes lead to flights of wealth, may partly explain this. But so too may the sheer political power of wealth. Whatever the reason it is a stark reminder that taxing wealth properly will not be easy.

Promises by the new Conservative government in the UK to raise the threshold for inheritance tax on the value of owner occupied homes and the new ability to hand on unused pension capital to one's children will further reduce the yield of these taxes and increase the growing scale of inherited wealth.

So what are the options for reversing these trends? It is clear that a range of measures will be needed in combination. Different kinds of wealth require different tax measures.

About half of net wealth in the UK takes the form of property and land. Taxing this sensibly would bring economic benefits. Land is given. It is not (mostly) created by human effort. Its value is largely created by public action – building roads, putting in sewers and properly policing the urban areas created. Value is created by the state giving planning permission to develop. Here there is a case for a range of potential reforms.

A site value tax – a percentage tax on land above a minimum value – would ensure that when an owner of a plot of land was given planning permission to develop, tax would be levied on the new market value that has been generated by granting planning permission. This would encourage its timely development. It would bring future tax benefits to the state and facilitate infrastructure schemes. Town planning rules do enable limited, one off agreements for developers to make planning gain payments at present but this would be automatic under a reformed tax regime. Such taxes exist in some other countries including Denmark, parts of the USA and Australia. (The Mirrlees Review lucidly argued that the whole system of property taxation in the UK was an illogical and inequitable mess.)

There should be no exclusions, such as forests or owner-occupied houses. Such loop holes only encourage over investment as a way of avoiding taxes, pushing up the price of houses, for example. The state has good data on who owns land. We also have good data on sales values to make valuation and regular revaluation much easier than it was in pre-digital days.

This proposal, however, would have a knock-on effect on council tax. It would be unpopular and inefficient to have two taxes levied on the same house – a major source of unpopularity around the proposed mansion tax. As such, council tax could be replaced by a tax on the value of the buildings, paid by the occupier and service user – distinguished from the value of the land, paid by the owner. This would be technically feasible using the valuations for building insurance.

Another option would be to replace council tax with a local income tax. Those with incomes below the tax threshold would effectively have their tax paid by central government and the local authority could be compensated by the central government grant. There are obstacles to this route – high income residents moving to low tax areas – but the logic of replacing the council tax flows from introducing a site value tax as the Mirrlees Review argued.

Next in line could be the full taxation of capital gains, at the same rate as income tax and employee national insurance contributions taken together.

Capital gains should also be taxed prior to assessing inheritance. Nor should owner-occupied property escape capital gains entirely. Not to tax it has resulted in people using housing as a way of preserving their wealth. This practice would only increase if other forms of wealth were effectively taxed.

This results in higher house prices, excluding those on lower incomes from the housing market.

Pension assets are another major source of wealth and one that is perversely subsidised by the general tax payer – the higher your income the greater the tax subsidy. A reduced cap has been placed on this subsidy but there is a long way to go, and there may be a case for tax encouragement for small savers but not rich ones.

The boundary line between capital and income for tax purposes has also been eroded, providing potential avenues of reform. It is possible for directors of companies to limit their tax liabilities by taking their income in the form of capital gains and dividends which are taxed at a lower rate than income. One way would be to revert to the regime that applied between 1988 and 1998 with real (after inflation) capital gains taxed at the same rate as an individual's marginal income. Returns on investment above a given 'normal rate' could be taxed like any other income, as the Mirrlees Review suggested.

So far I have avoided what some see as the obvious solution, including Thomas Piketty – an annual tax on all personal assets. Labour's 1974 election manifesto promised to introduce such a tax, but did not do so upon election. Contemporary Treasury and Inland Revenue files suggested they were right to do so, as my research has shown.[4] This was because the cost to individuals and government of valuing wealth assets annually, with concurrent Inland Revenue checks, out-weighed much of the likely revenue yield, not to mention the difficult science of calculating the appreciation of wealth's value.

Moreover, there is a better way and it has been advocated by Piketty's mentor Sir Tony Atkinson and others including John Stuart Mill. Instead of having the state impose a compulsory asset and wealth tax, principally at the point of death, we should give individuals and families the choice of how to use their wealth, while strongly incentivising them to spread their wealth widely. The best way to do this is to tax recipients, via an accessions or donee tax.

In this model, gifts or transfers over a minimum sum would be taxed – initial small sums could be excluded but as gifts mounted over a period they would be taxed. Gifts to properly defined charities would be excluded.

There are difficulties with this arrangement, of course. Revenue from inheritance tax is currently rather small, but under this model it would disappear completely. However, if this model worked, its virtue would be that accumulated wealth would not steadily accumulate in fewer and fewer hands.

There are therefore a range of different, complementary and achievable options open to us. But fundamentally, it is not enough to try to reallocate wealth merely through taxation. These reforms should be accompanied and justified by promoting wealth at the bottom of the wealth distribution, through schemes such as reintroducing the Child Trust Fund – giving all citizens at the age of 18 a capital start in life. We also need to invest in early years education, offering most citizens a greater opportunity to generate wealth themselves starting from a more levelled playing field. The more effectively we can tax wealth, the bigger the opportunity we have to invest in everyone's life chances, helping create the fairer society and more efficient economy that should appeal to a broad electorate.

Notes

1. These figures and others in this chapter are taken from Hills J., Bastagli F., Cowell F., Glennerster H., Karagiannaki and McKnight, A. *Wealth in the UK: Distribution, Accumulation and Policy* Oxford: Oxford University Press 2015 (paperback edition.).
2. 'Wealth Inequality and the Accumulation of Debt' in W.Salverda, B.Nolan, D.Checchi, I.Marx, A.Mcknight, I.G.Toth and H. van de Werfhorst *Changing Inequalities in Rich Countries* Oxford: Oxford University Press.
3. 'Trends in the Distribution of Wealth in Britain' in Hills et al 2015 op.cit.
4. H.Glennerster 'Why Was a Wealth Tax for the UK abandoned? Lessons for the Policy Process and Tackling Wealth Inequality' *Journal of Social Policy* Vol 41 P 2 pp 233–249, 2012.

8: POORLY TARGETED: REFORMING THE TAXATION OF LOW INCOME FAMILIES

Adam Corlett

Recent reforms have focused on raising the personal allowance to 'take the poorest out of tax', but this is not the progressive policy it purports to be. If we want to genuinely support lower income households, we need to engage with reforming a broad range of different taxes as well as looking to the much bigger prize of the benefits system.

Often in discussions of inequality, 'progressive' politics and 'fairness', the debates around tax are dominated by how we should tax those at the top. But it's just as important to look at the people this is supposed to be helping. This means considering how taxes could be reformed to help low and middle income families directly,[1] as well as what limits there are to helping them through the tax system.

Recent debates on tackling tax evasion and calls for new taxes on the richest are welcome, but from the perspective of low earning families, their *direct* relevance is limited. At the same time, there has been great emphasis on raising the 'tax free' personal allowance for income tax – sold as 'taking the poorest out of tax' and a 'tax cut for low earners'. This represents a shift from discussing cutting rates to raising allowances, which is far more helpful for the poorer half of society. However, while very popular, it is not as progressive as proponents often argue (and note that the same applies to the very similar policy of reintroducing a 10p band).

First, almost all income taxpayers benefit from the policy, which makes it very expensive and not well targeted, with most of the gains going to the top half of income groups. Furthermore, as ever more taxpayers are already 'taken out' of tax, there are diminishing returns for the poorest income groups. Finally, income tax is not such a large part of the tax paid by low income families, representing only 19 per cent of their total tax burden on average.[2]

So, if we want to reform taxation in a way that genuinely supports lower income households, we need to engage with reforming the broad range of different taxes that make up the bulk of the low income tax burden.

Making tax fairer for the poorest

First, there's income tax's ugly and criminally-neglected sister: National Insurance (NI). This kicks in at around £8,000 while the income tax allowance for 2015–16 is £10,600. This means there are around 1.5 million low earners who have been 'taken out of tax' but still pay NI. Realigning these thresholds, and therefore abolishing a 12 per cent tax band for the lowest paid, should be a greater priority than further income tax cuts, though it would again be higher income households who would benefit most.

Indeed, the existence of a separate NI system now seems more of a burden than an ally for poorer households. NI more generally is unhelpful in achieving 'vertical' or 'horizontal' tax equity and transparency; that is people in similar circumstances pay similar amounts, and that the better-off pay at least the same proportion as the less well-off. For decades, governments have cut income tax while increasing NI. The result is that if your money comes from owning property or stocks, you pay income tax at 20 per cent, but if your money comes from employment, you pay a combined rate of 32 per cent (even before considering 13.8 per cent employer NI – which arguably lowers salaries). Similarly, the regressive structure of NI, with the rate falling from 12 per cent to 2 per cent at higher incomes (and a flat rate for employer NI), means that the progression of tax rates is not as steep as the headline income tax rates suggest, providing a further progressive case for reform.

Even more of a burden for lower income families is VAT, which makes up 23 per cent of their overall tax burden on average. This is a greater proportion than either income tax or NI, despite the fact that many goods and services are exempted or subject to lower rates (the UK having one of the narrowest VAT bases in the EU). Similarly, the impact of corporation tax and business rates may be passed onto consumers through prices or employees through lower wages. But there are strong arguments in favour of keeping all of these taxes, and of avoiding frequent changes. So given the expense of cutting these economy-wide taxes, better targeted approaches need to be found.

Perhaps surprisingly, taxes on alcohol, cigarettes and transport are together roughly as significant for poorer households as income tax, at 17 per cent of their tax bill on average. Of course, such 'sin' taxes are deliberately high, but any opportunity to reduce this burden should be explored – demonstrating the links between tax and other areas of public policy. For example, a big reduction in smoking, such as due to a wholesale shift to e-cigarettes (assuming that they are far less unhealthy than tobacco), would be an extremely significant tax cut for low and middle income families, more so than many of the tax cuts that are bandied around. The long-term need to reform fuel duty and Vehicle Excise Duty (despite recent changes to the latter) to reflect the greening of cars may also present opportunities to make these taxes more progressive while maintaining their behavioural and revenue-raising goals.

Finally, there's council tax, which makes up 13 per cent of the poorer half's taxes (before considering benefits), offering one of the clearest opportunities to make the tax system fairer for lower income families, through both revaluation and reform of tax bands. Partially inheriting its design from the poll tax, council tax is unusual in being deliberately regressive. A property worth hundreds of times more than another may nonetheless incur a maximum of three times the tax. As Paul Johnson puts it, "We wouldn't charge a lower rate of VAT on a Ferrari than on a Nissan. It is not much more evident why we should charge a lower rate of council tax on a £2 million mansion than on a £50,000 flat."

Together with the fact that it is based on property values as they stood in 1991, and that this is likely to still be the case in 2021, it is ripe for reform. Many of the UK's neighbours offer examples for reform. Ireland has moved to a system that uses bands but is proportional (except at the top where the tax rate actually increases). In the Netherlands, properties are revalued every year and are taxed at a flat rate set by each municipality. And in Norway, municipalities can tax property at up to 0.7 per cent of value. If these and many other countries can manage it, why can't the UK?

In the recent general election, Labour and the Liberal Democrats both proposed extra council tax bands – or their equivalent – at the top of the system. But there is a need for more bands at the bottom too, as demonstrated by the fact that in the north of England and the midlands, 42 per cent of households are lumped together in Band A, as Resolution Foundation analysis has shown. A limited reform (but still ambitious given the past 25 years) would be a revaluation with new bands or a percentage charge at the top, funding at least one extra band towards the bottom. The goal – whether achieved incrementally or in one, and nationally or via devolution – should be to move closer towards a tax that would be around 0.5 to 0.6 per cent of the up-to-date property value each year (so, for example, a £100,000 home would pay £500–£600).[3]

Raising revenue

So, there are some limited opportunities and longstanding possibilities to reduce taxes for low and middle income families. And there are some ways to fund those within the same taxes, but – to take a brief look at the taxes of those on higher incomes – how else might revenue be raised?

One critical yet achievable goal would be better scrutiny of tax breaks. These are often well-intentioned, designed to support growth or fix a wrong elsewhere in the system, though cynics might suggest many have more to do with winning votes or simply historical accident. But assessment of whether these tax expenditures are meeting their goals is limited at best, and incomparable to the scrutiny that spending programmes receive, despite their equivalent budgetary impact.

These tax breaks might be incentives to encourage business creation (such as loopholes in capital gains tax or inheritance tax); the differing NI treatment of different sources of income, as discussed above; pension and age-related tax breaks (such as the NI exemption for older workers); or the favourable treatment of property ownership. Some go to the top 1 per cent or 10 per cent; others to those on high but not super-high incomes. Most importantly, none are well targeted at the bottom. And while they may have benefits – and we should seek a tax system that supports long-term productivity growth, employment, economic stability and homebuilding – it's worth asking whether these tens of billions of pounds per year could be better and more evenly dispersed. As William Gladstone put it in 1863, "in every case exemption means a relief to A at the charge of B". In effect "B" is usually the typical low or middle income employee. So we need to improve both the formal scrutiny and informal discourse around tax breaks, while also laying out the size of the potential prize: how else could taxes be cut for the same cost?

The limits of conventional tax cuts

However, there are limits to what can be done through the tax system. On direct taxes, 43 per cent of adults already pay no income tax[4] (though some of those pay NI), and it is arguably even harder to target indirect tax cuts on poorer families, meaning the potential for boosting their incomes through cheap tax cuts is limited.

The benefit system, on the other hand, works very well at targeting low and middle income families – and even universal benefits are more progressive than almost any tax cut. The introduction of universal credit is a good chance to consider the importance of the benefits system. It will cover around a third of working-age households, including half of all children, and a large number will face a withdrawal rate (with their benefit being reduced as earnings increase) of 65 per cent, which when combined with direct taxes will most often mean a 76 per cent effective tax rate. What's more, and in a change from the current benefits system, two thirds of any gains from income tax and NI cuts will now, just like extra earnings, be withdrawn from universal credit households.

From a low income perspective, ensuring the benefits system works as well as possible therefore offers a much bigger prize than tweaking the tax system, as the Resolution Foundation's recent review of universal credit has shown.

However, although out-of-work welfare reliance is at its lowest level since the 1970s at least,[5] "hand-outs" will never be particularly popular with the public. On the other hand, tax cuts are extremely popular. So to ensure continued (or even increased) support for lower income families, one answer might be to rebrand or reform benefit giveaways as tax cuts.

For economists, at least, the two aren't particularly different. Consider, for example, council tax support, which provides a discount to council tax: is that a benefit or a tax cut? Many would say it's clearly a tax reduction – and indeed there have been campaigns to rename it as a tax 'rebate' – but it is not counted as such. The distinction is important for public perceptions, and for the numerical size of 'the state' and the 'welfare budget', even if it makes no difference to disposable incomes.

Similarly, under the tax credit system, the benefit was recorded as a tax cut for those paying income tax and as 'spending' for those not. We should consider extending this idea within universal credit. It's fairly common to be paying thousands of pounds in income tax and employee NI, and another thousand in council tax, while also receiving similar amounts in benefits. It would not be affordable to cut taxes so far for everyone that no one on universal credit would face taxes. But instead of both receiving benefits and paying tax, would it not be possible to deliver universal credit (or child benefit, or others) as a cut to your income tax, employee NI, and council tax, with only the remainder delivered as a 'benefit'? None of this would directly change people's incomes or work incentives, and it would require significant administrative change. But it could change people's perceptions of our entire tax and benefit systems and whether they or others deserved support. More broadly, beyond the taxes that can be directly cancelled out, one could paint a large proportion of – though certainly not all of – welfare spending as effectively tax rebates (or prebates) for VAT and other indirect taxes. Again, discourse should reflect the fact that the benefits system and tax system do not exist in isolation.

There are therefore tax reforms that would help low and middle income families, and many more if we cast our nets only a little further to the deeply linked benefits system. While much recent rhetoric has focused on ostensibly popular but relatively poorly targeted changes to income tax, a broader programme of reforming and reframing taxes and benefits could have a far greater impact. If we want to see truly progressive tax reforms focused on the bottom half, political bravery and determination will be essential.

Notes

1. Taken here to mean the poorer half of households.
2. For the poorest half of non-retired households. This and other figures (all excluding retired households) from ONS, *The effects of taxes and benefits on household income, financial year ending 2014* (2015).
3. J Mirrlees et al., *Tax by design*, IFS, September 2011 & A Atkinson, I*nequality: What can be done?*, April 2015.
4. S Adam et al., *Taxes and benefits: the parties' plans*, IFS, April 2015
5. P Gregg & A Corlett, *An ocean apart: the US-UK switch in employment and benefit receipt*, Resolution Foundation, June 2015.

Discussion Guide: Tax for our Times

How to use this Discussion Guide

The guide can be used in various ways by Fabian Local Societies, local political party meetings and trade union branches, student societies, NGOs and other groups.

- You might hold a discussion among local members or invite a guest speaker – for example, an MP, academic or local practitioner to lead a group discussion.
- Some different key themes are suggested. You might choose to spend 15–20 minutes on each area, or decide to focus the whole discussion on one of the issues for a more detailed discussion.